Things with Wings

THE LIFE CYCLE OF A CICADA

by JoAnn Early Macken

Reading consultant: Susan Nations, M.Ed.,
author/literacy coach/consultant in literacy development

Please visit our web site at: www.earlyliteracy.cc
For a free color catalog describing Weekly Reader® Early Learning Library's
list of high-quality books, call 1-877-445-5824 (USA) or 1-800-387-3178 (Canada).
Weekly Reader® Early Learning Library's fax: (414) 336-0164.

Library of Congress Cataloging-in-Publication Data

Macken, JoAnn Early, 1953-
    The life cycle of a cicada / by JoAnn Early Macken.
      p. cm. — (Things with wings)
    Includes index.
    ISBN 0-8368-6380-1 (lib. bdg.)
    ISBN 0-8368-6387-9 (softcover)
    1. Cicadas—Life cycles—Juvenile literature.   I. Title.
QL527.C5M33   2006
595.7'52—dc22   2005026540

This edition first published in 2006 by
Weekly Reader® Early Learning Library
A Member of the WRC Media Family of Companies
330 West Olive Street, Suite 100
Milwaukee, WI 53212 USA

Managing editor: Dorothy L. Gibbs
Art direction: Tammy West
Photo research: Diane Laska-Swanke

Photo credits: Cover, pp. 11, 13, 17, 21 © James P. Rowan; pp. 5, 7, 9 © Michael J. Raupp,
Professor of Entomology, University of Maryland in College Park; p. 15 © Richard Day/Daybreak
Imagery; p. 19 © Gary Meszaros/Visuals Unlimited

Printed in the United States of America

1 2 3 4 5 6 7 8 9 10 09 08 07 06

Note to Educators and Parents

Reading is such an exciting adventure for young children! They are beginning to integrate their oral language skills with written language. To encourage children along the path to early literacy, books must be colorful, engaging, and interesting; they should invite the young reader to explore both the print and the pictures.

Things with Wings is a new series designed to help children read about fascinating animals, all of which have wings. In each book, young readers will learn about the life cycle of the featured animal, as well as other interesting facts.

Each book is specially designed to support the young reader in the reading process. The familiar topics are appealing to young children and invite them to read — and re-read — again and again. The full-color photographs and enhanced text further support the student during the reading process.

In addition to serving as wonderful picture books in schools, libraries, homes, and other places where children learn to love reading, these books are specifically intended to be read within an instructional guided reading group. This small group setting allows beginning readers to work with a fluent adult model as they make meaning from the text. After children develop fluency with the text and content, the book can be read independently. Children and adults alike will find these books supportive, engaging, and fun!

— Susan Nations, M.Ed., author, literacy coach, and consultant in literacy development

A cicada (sih KAY dah) begins life as an egg. When the egg hatches, a **nymph** will come out. A nymph is a young insect.

egg

5

Cicada eggs often hatch in trees. Soon, the nymphs drop to the ground and dig into the ground.

nymph

7

Under the ground, nymphs drink **sap**, or juice, from plant roots. Some kinds stay under the ground for one or two years. Some stay for thirteen years. Others stay for seventeen years!

nymph

9

A cicada can take a long time to grow. As it grows, it sheds its skin, or **molts**.

11

When a cicada is grown, it digs its way out of the ground. It climbs onto a tree or some other plant. Then it molts for the last time.

13

An adult cicada has two pairs of wings. Like all insects, it has six legs. It has two large eyes and three small ones.

Most cicadas are black. Some are green or yellow. Many have green marks on their bodies. Some have red eyes.

17

Male cicadas sing to find mates. They sing when the weather is warm. Their song sounds like a buzz. It can be loud!

Adult cicadas live only a few weeks. They suck sap from trees. Female cicadas lay eggs in trees. In a few weeks, the eggs hatch.

The Life Cycle of a Cicada

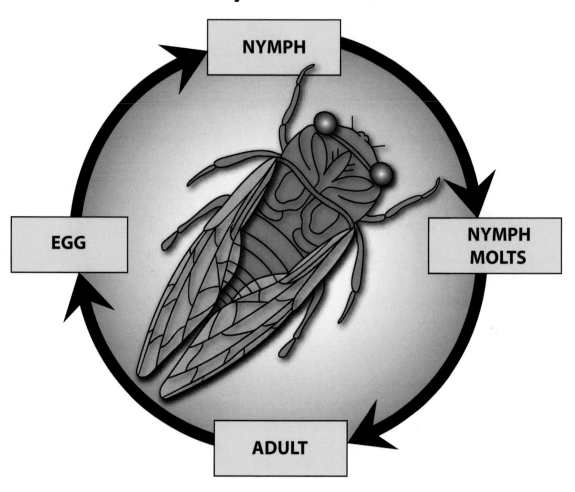

NYMPH

EGG

NYMPH MOLTS

ADULT

Glossary

hatches — breaks out of an egg

molts — sheds, or loses, the skin

nymph — young insect

sap — juice from trees or other plants

Index

About the Author

JoAnn Early Macken is the author of two rhyming picture books, *Sing-Along Song* and *Cats on Judy*, and more than eighty nonfiction books for children. Her poems have appeared in several children's magazines. A graduate of the M.F.A. in Writing for Children and Young Adults Program at Vermont College, she lives in Wisconsin with her husband and their two sons.